Jesus is
No Secret

Carolyn Nystrom

ILLUSTRATED BY EIRA REEVES

Text © 1981 by The Moody Bible
Institute of Chicago
Design © 1993 Three's Company,
London

First published in this edition by
Moody Press in 1994

ISBN: 0−8024−7865−4
Designed and created by
Three's Company, 12 Flitcroft Street,
London WC2H 8DJ
Worldwide co-edition organized and
produced by Angus Hudson Ltd,
Concorde House, Grenville Place,
London NW7 3SA

Printed in Singapore

Moody Press, a ministry of the Moody
Bible Institute, is designed for
education, evangelization, and
edification. If we may assist you in
knowing more about Christ and the
Christian life, please write us without
obligation: Moody Press, c/o MLM,
Chicago, Illinois, 60610.

Do you like to talk about Jesus?
I do.

I am a Christian, so Jesus is very important to me. Of course I want to talk about Him.

But talking about Jesus doesn't always work out the way I plan. Last week I was climbing a tree with Brad. I said, "Brad, you should be a Christian. If you aren't, you won't go to heaven. You should come to my church so you can learn about Jesus."

But Brad got mad. He said, "You think you're better than anybody else just because you go to church. Going to church doesn't make anybody a Christian."

Brad's mom was mad, too. She wouldn't let him play with me for a whole week.

4

I didn't want to make all of my friends mad at me, so I wondered, *Should I talk about Jesus to just anyone? Or should I talk about Jesus only at home and at church? Is Jesus a secret?*

5

Later I told my mom about Brad. "I'm sorry Brad got angry." Mom looked sad. "Not everyone wants to hear about Jesus. But Brad is right about one thing," Mom went on. "Going to church doesn't make anybody a Christian."

Then Mom explained. "Do you remember when you became a Christian last year?"

I nodded.

"How did it happen? Do you remember the three steps?"

Isaiah 59:1–2; 1 John 1:9

Slowly I repeated them:
"*Think.* I thought of the things I had done wrong.

Acts 16:30–31

"*Believe.* I believed that Jesus died and came back to life to forgive those sins and take them away forever.

Romans 10:9–10

"*Decide.* I decided that I wanted to belong to Jesus and let him be in charge of everything that I do."

8

"I remember what you prayed then," Mom added. "You said, 'Jesus, I give You myself.'"

"I remember what I was thinking." I laughed. "I thought of myself wrapped up with a great big red bow as a present for Jesus."

Romans 12:1–2

"But now I know that giving myself to Jesus means more than a present with a bow. It means that I will try hard to do all the things that Jesus teaches in the Bible. It's like Jesus is my boss. But He loves me, and I love Him. So He's also my friend."

Hebrews 5:8–10; Hebrews 10:25

"But what about church?" I asked. "Don't Christians go to church?"

"Yes," answered Mom. "You probably learned how to become a Christian in church. But church didn't save you. Jesus did."

11

I learned other things about Jesus that day. Jesus does not want to be a secret. After Jesus had taught His twelve special friends for a while, He sent them out to tell others about Him. Jesus told them to help people the way He had and to teach people the wise things He had been teaching them.

"But not everyone will want to hear about Me," Jesus warned His friends. "Some of them will hate you and maybe even try to hurt you. But do not be afraid. Others will learn to love Me just as much as you do. They will become part of God's family with you."

The Bible

The BIBLE

13

Matthew 28:16–20

Later, when Jesus was about to leave and go back to His Father in heaven, He told all of His friends, "Go into all the world, teach people in every country all that I have taught you. Help people everywhere to give themselves to Me."

MAP OF THE WORLD

Jesus promised that when He was in heaven He would send the Holy Spirit to live in each person who belonged to Him. The Holy Spirit would give every Christian special power to tell others about Jesus in ways they could understand.

God wants even those who are young to share the good news He gives them. Long ago, the prophet Jeremiah complained, "O Lord God, I do not know how to talk about You; I am only a child."

But God answered, "Do not be afraid. I am with you. I will take care of you. I have put My words in your mouth."

Hundreds of years later, the apostle Paul told his young friend Timothy, "Don't be embarrassed to talk about Jesus. Jesus has loved you from the beginning of time. And He gives you life in heaven with Him forever."

17

Acts 13:1—3; Acts 15:40—16:5

Paul was the first Christian missionary. Paul's church sent him and a friend on three long trips. They traveled on boats over the sea, and they walked hundreds of miles over the land. Everywhere they went, they told people about Jesus.

Not everyone believed what Paul told them, but some of them did. Paul helped those new believers get together and form churches.

When Paul was allowed to speak to large groups, he always talked about Jesus. Sometimes he told how he had met Jesus. People always seemed interested when he talked about that. It was like hearing a story.

Maybe I should tell Brad how I became a Christian.

PAUL'S ADVENTURES

2 Corinthians 5:14—21

Later Paul wrote, "It is the love of Jesus that keeps me telling others about Him. It's as if Jesus is speaking through me to bring people to God."

Today missionaries still travel far away to share Jesus with people who have never heard about Him. They travel on boats and planes and jeeps and burros and even on foot. They work in crowded cities, and high mountains, and deep forests, and lonely deserts.

God can use all kinds of workers as missionaries. Some missionaries are doctors or nurses or teachers. Others study languages and copy the Bible so people can read it for the first time. Missionaries fly airplanes to carry mail and food and move sick people to hospitals. Missionaries even repair motorcycles so they can travel rough trails where cars can't go. But whatever he or she does, a missionary shares the good news of Jesus.

25

Not everyone can travel far away to do mission work. I have to stay home with my family and go to school. But everyone can help missionaries in some way:

My Sunday school class made a picture book to help missionaries teach other children to read.

My family sends letters and pictures to our friends who are missionaries. We know that sometimes they get lonely and miss us. I send a note, too.

Pray for the Elvin family

Sometimes we pack a box of special gifts wrapped in pretty paper. We try to put in things the missionaries can't buy where they live. Then we mail it in time for Christmas or a birthday.

We can send money to missionaries. I give some of my allowance.

And we can all pray for missionaries. We know that sometimes their work is hard and dangerous. They need special help from God.

When missionaries come back to our country, they often don't have a place to live. Their home and friends are far away. We invite them to stay at our house for a while. I share my clothes and toys, and I introduce the children to my friends.

Missions is a job for all Christians. God wants all of us to have some part in spreading the good news of Jesus.

I still wish Brad knew about Jesus. I like Brad, and I want to be his friend. Friends share the good things they have with each other. Maybe I can show Brad that Jesus loves him even more than I do. Then we will share the best Friend of all.

When I'm older, I'll think about working as a missionary. But whatever job I do, even if I stay close to home, I will still talk about Jesus. Jesus is no secret.